Happiness is …

The best of the Hamlet moments

BLOOMSBURY

First published in Great Britain 1993

Bloomsbury Publishing Limited, 2 Soho Square, London W1V 5DE

Compilation copyright © 1993 by Gallaher Limited

Introduction copyright © 1993 by William Rushton

Cartoon Credits

Caldwell: Hamlet moments 1, 42, 59, 102, 103, 110. **CDP/Noel Ford**: Hamlet moment 82.
CDP/Gray Joliffe: Hamlet moments 46, 47, 83, 84. **CDP/McLachlan**: Hamlet moment 81. **'Danny'**: Hamlet moment 96.
de la Nougerede: Hamlet moments 16, 92. **Pat Drennan**: Hamlet moments 28, 65, 66, 67, 87. **Emms**: Hamlet moment 49.
Fiddy: Hamlet moments 5, 26, 62, 69. **Noel Ford**: Hamlet moments 19, 101, 104. **Haldane**: Hamlet moments 15, 20, 64, 90, 91, 99.
Julie Hollings: Hamlet moment 79. **'Holte'**: Hamlet moments 80, 107. **'Larry'**: Hamlet moments 10, 24, 55, 100.
McLachlan: Hamlet moments 2,13, 23, 52, 74, 75, 78. **David Myers**: Hamlet moments 9, 30, 31, 60, 70.
'Sax': Hamlet moments 35, 38, 40, 41, 85, 88, 95. **Mike Williams**: Hamlet moments 76, 114.

All other cartoons courtesy of CDP.

A CIP catalogue record for this book is available from the British Library

ISBN 0 7475 1579 4

Front cover cartoon by Pat Drennan
Designed by Fielding Rowinski
Printed by The Bath Press, Avon

Introduction

It is said that every comedian wants to play Hamlet. I have always had serious doubts about this. It's far too much to remember, for one, and contains very few laughs. (Actually not having to get laughs is quite relaxing, so there may be an element of truth there.) I shall start again. It would be fair to say that very few comedians would not have given their comedy teeth to have appeared in a Hamlet commercial. I was reminded how good they were when putting them all (or most of them) together in a video to mourn their passing on TV. It's hard to believe that the first one appeared on telly in 1964. In black and white. And in many parts of the country, silent. Like so much of my early career.

The best thing about Hamlet commercials is that we know the feeling. Bored. Frustrated. At risk, perhaps. In pain. Then that chord from Jacques Loussier. . . and sod it, so what? Puff, puff. All human life is there.

It was a sad day – it usually is – when Nanny struck and the commercials were no more. But this book is evidence of the resilience of the human spirit. Up they popped as cartoons on hoardings and in newspapers. There are some unforgettable ones in here too. That Hamlet moment is well known to all of us.

One thing I don't understand, Inspector, in none of the commercials and nowhere in this book has the eponymous Hamlet appeared. I can see the gloomy Dane on an Elsinore battlement ... "To be, or not to be ... Oh sod it!" Ping! and lighting up.

Thank you, Hamlet,

William Rushton.

HAMLET MOMENT

HAMLET MOMENT

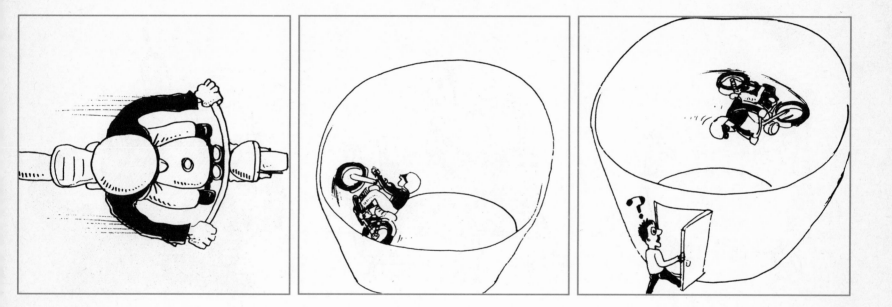

HAMLET MOMENT

HAMLET MOMENT

HAMLET MOMENT

HAMLET MOMENT

HAMLET MOMENT

HAMLET MOMENT

From an idea by George Bayliss

HAMLET MOMENT
···

10

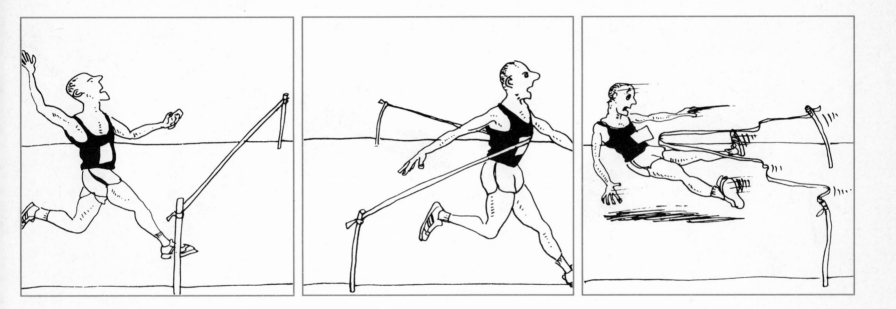

HAMLET MOMENT

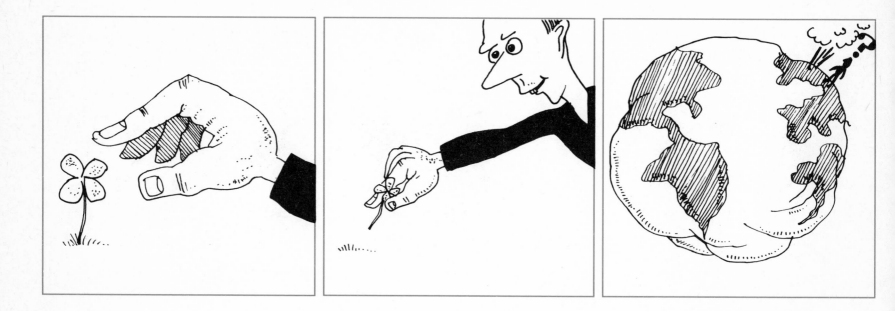

HAMLET MOMENT

HAMLET MOMENT

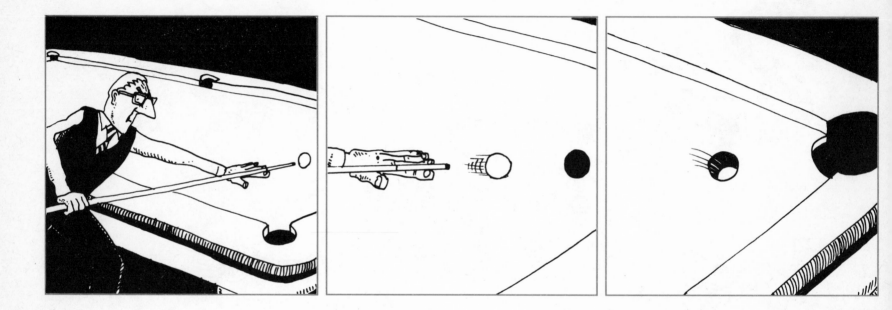

HAMLET MOMENT

HAMLET MOMENT

In the illustration: "Treatise on the Theory of Gravity by Isaac Newton"

de la Nougerede

From an idea by Dale Robinson

HAMLET MOMENT

16

HAMLET MOMENT

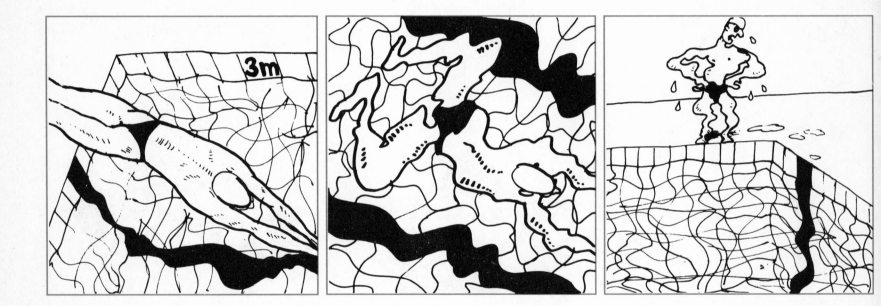

HAMLET MOMENT

HAMLET MOMENT

HAMLET MOMENT

HAMLET MOMENT

HAMLET MOMENT

HAMLET MOMENT

HAMLET MOMENT

HAMLET MOMENT

HAMLET MOMENT

HAMLET MOMENT

From an idea by Tony Doe

HAMLET MOMENT

28

HAMLET MOMENT

HAMLET MOMENT

HAMLET MOMENT

HAMLET MOMENT

HAMLET MOMENT

HAMLET MOMENT

From an idea by Claire Brown

HAMLET MOMENT

HAMLET MOMENT

HAMLET MOMENT

From an idea by S. Nelson

HAMLET MOMENT

HAMLET MOMENT

HAMLET MOMENT

HAMLET MOMENT

HAMLET MOMENT

HAMLET MOMENT

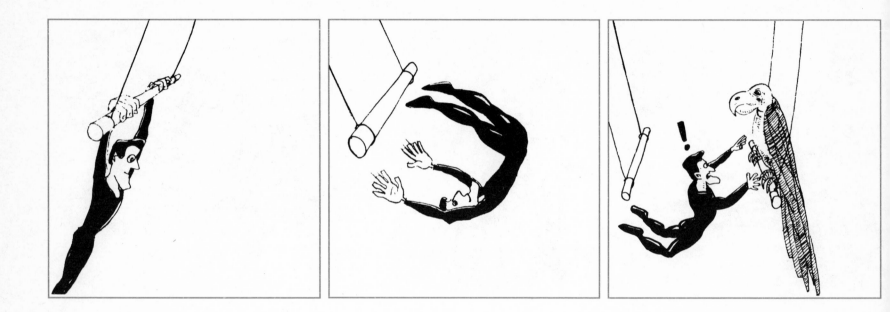

HAMLET MOMENT

HAMLET MOMENT

HAMLET MOMENT

HAMLET MOMENT

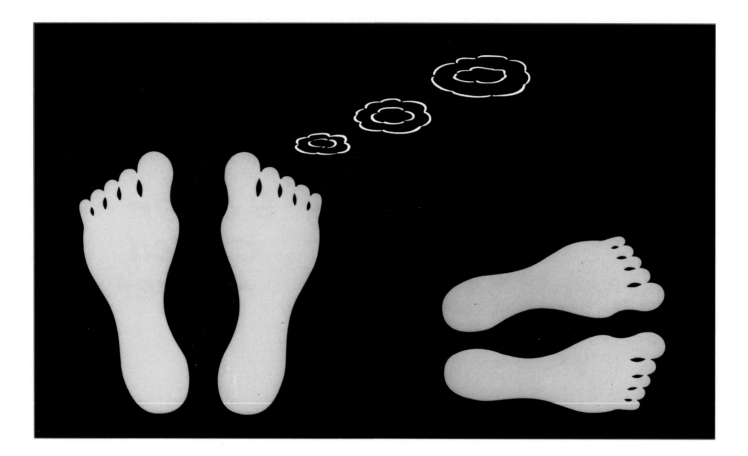

HAMLET MOMENT

HAMLET MOMENT

HAMLET MOMENT

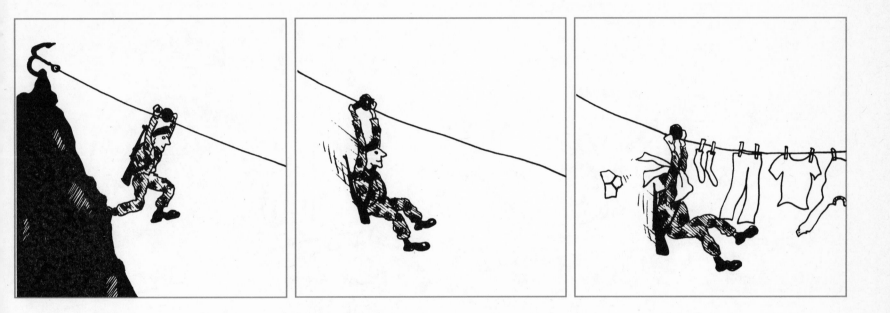

HAMLET MOMENT

HAMLET MOMENT

HAMLET MOMENT

HAMLET MOMENT

HAMLET MOMENT

HAMLET MOMENT

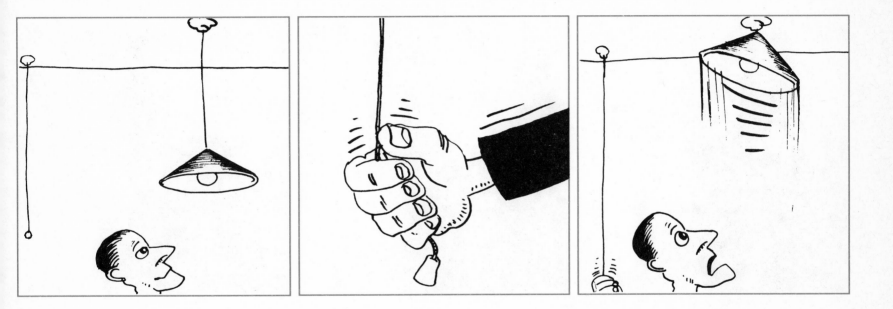

HAMLET MOMENT

HAMLET MOMENT

HAMLET MOMENT

From an idea by W.A. Edwards

HAMLET MOMENT

HAMLET MOMENT

HAMLET MOMENT

HAMLET MOMENT

HAMLET MOMENT

HAMLET MOMENT

From an idea by L.G. Largent

HAMLET MOMENT

From an idea by A.C. Hawkins

HAMLET MOMENT

HAMLET MOMENT

HAMLET MOMENT

HAMLET MOMENT

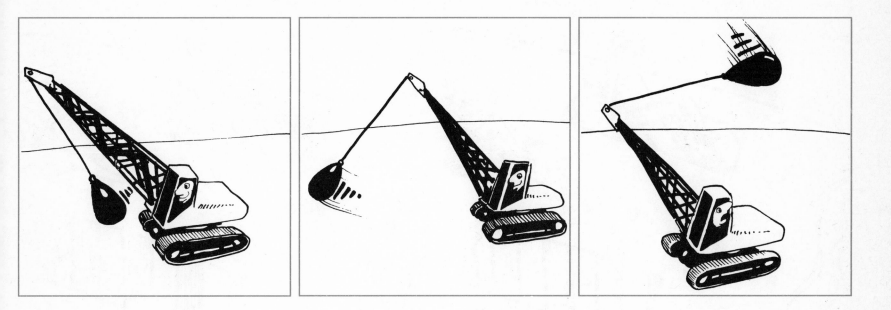

HAMLET MOMENT

HAMLET MOMENT

Happiness is a cigar called Hamlet.

HAMLET MOMENT

HAMLET MOMENT

HAMLET MOMENT

HAMLET MOMENT

HAMLET MOMENT

HAMLET MOMENT

From an idea by R. Wood

HAMLET MOMENT

HAMLET MOMENT

HAMLET MOMENT

Happiness is a cigar called Hamlet

Happiness is a cigar called Hamlet

From an idea by B.R. Friendship

HAMLET MOMENT

HAMLET MOMENT

HAMLET MOMENT

From an idea by Timothy Thouless

HAMLET MOMENT

HAMLET MOMENT

HAMLET MOMENT

HAMLET MOMENT

From an idea by Ann Workman

HAMLET MOMENT

92

HAMLET MOMENT

HAMLET MOMENT

HAMLET MOMENT

From an idea by S.L. Brompton

HAMLET MOMENT

· ·

HAMLET MOMENT

HAMLET MOMENT

HAMLET MOMENT

HAMLET MOMENT

HAMLET MOMENT

HAMLET MOMENT

From an idea by G. Monaghan

HAMLET MOMENT

· ·

HAMLET MOMENT

From an idea by Ivan

HAMLET MOMENT

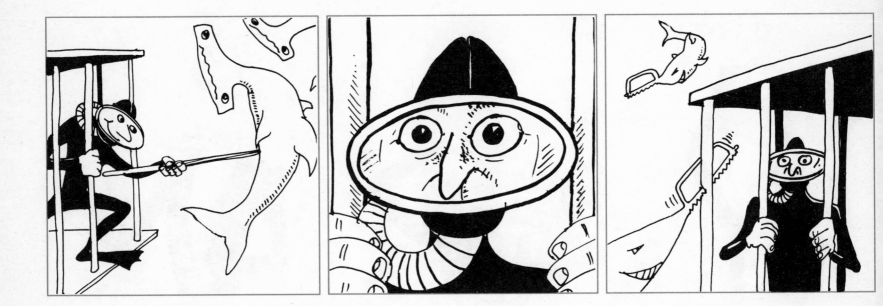

HAMLET MOMENT

HAMLET MOMENT

HAMLET MOMENT

HAMLET MOMENT

HAMLET MOMENT

HAMLET MOMENT

HAMLET MOMENT

HAMLET MOMENT

Happiness is... £5,000

Hamlet cigars have become a household name through television, radio, poster and newspaper commercials depicting typical Hamlet moments. Now you have the chance to create your own Hamlet moment. Simply send your cartoon idea with your name and address to

Hamlet Cartoon Competition, PO Box 122, Uckfield X, East Sussex TN22 5UU

Each month from November 1993 to April 1994 we will judge the entries, and the one that is most apt and amusing will win £100 and be put forward into our grand final with a chance to win £5,000.

Rules of Entry

1. Each £100 prize will be awarded to the entrant who, in the opinion of the judges, has submitted the most apt and amusing Hamlet moment during the previous month. No entrant may win more than one £100 prize.

2. You may enter as many times as you like. The £5,000 prize will be awarded to the most apt and amusing entry out of the monthly winners.

3. Responsibility will not be accepted for entries lost, delayed, mislaid or damaged in the post or offered for delivery insufficiently stamped. Proof of posting will not be accepted as proof of delivery.

4. All entries will automatically become the property of the Promoter and will not be returned. The Promoter reserves the right to use entries in publicity and promotional material including, without limitation, in a second edition of *Happiness Is* . . . and entrants are deemed to consent to any such use.

5. The competition is open only to UK resident smokers aged 18 or over, except the employees (and their families) of Benson & Hedges Ltd and Bloomsbury Publishing Ltd or anyone directly connected with the competition. By entering the competition all entrants will be deemed to have accepted and be bound by the Rules.

6. The judges' decision in respect of all matters relating to the competition shall be final and binding.

7. A list of prizewinners and their entries will be made available to those applying after 30th April 1994 to the competition address and enclosing an s.a.e.

8. All entries must be posted to the competition address.

9. Judging will take place on the first normal working business day of each month during the competition for all entries received since the previous judging date.

10. **The closing date for receipt of entries into the last month's competition is 31st March 1994.**

11. The Promoter is Benson & Hedges Ltd, 13 Old Bond Street, London, W1X 4QP. (Do not send entries to this address.)